J 921 LOV

SO-CWT-323

**Ada Lovelace : pioneering
computer
programming/"Doudna, Kelly"**

Dec 2018

33187004443673
FULTON COUNTY PUBLIC LIBRARY

Lexile: 810L

WITHDRAWN

Fulton Co. Public Library
320 W. 7th Street
Rochester, IN 46975

STEM
SUPERSTAR
WOMEN

ADA
LOVELACE

Pioneering Computer Programming

Kelly Doudna

Checkerboard
Library

An Imprint of Abdo Publishing
abdopublishing.com

abdopublishing.com

Published by Abdo Publishing, a division of ABDO, PO Box 398166, Minneapolis, Minnesota 55439. Copyright © 2018 by Abdo Consulting Group, Inc. International copyrights reserved in all countries. No part of this book may be reproduced in any form without written permission from the publisher. Checkerboard Library™ is a trademark and logo of Abdo Publishing.

Printed in the United States of America, North Mankato, Minnesota
102017
012018

THIS BOOK CONTAINS
RECYCLED MATERIALS

Design: Emily O'Malley, Mighty Media, Inc.
Production: Mighty Media, Inc.
Editor: Liz Salzmann
Cover Photograph: Wikimedia Commons
Interior Photographs: Alamy, pp. 5, 9, 24, 27; iStockphoto, p. 7; Jitze Couperus/Flickr, p. 15; moof/Flickr, p. 23; New York Public Library, pp. 13, 28 (right); Wikimedia Commons, pp. 11, 17, 19, 21, 28 (left), 29 (left and right)

Publisher's Cataloging-in-Publication Data
Names: Doudna, Kelly, author.
Title: Ada Lovelace: pioneering computer programming / by Kelly Doudna.
Other titles: Pioneering computer programming
Description: Minneapolis, Minnesota : Abdo Publishing, 2018. | Series: STEM superstar women | Includes online resources and index.
Identifiers: LCCN 2017944047 | ISBN 9781532112836 (lib.bdg.) | ISBN 9781532150555 (ebook)
Subjects: LCSH: Lovelace, Ada King, Countess of, 1815-1852--Juvenile literature. | Women mathematicians--Juvenile literature. | Women computer engineers--United States--Juvenile
    literature.
Classification: DDC 510.92 [B]--dc23
LC record available at https://lccn.loc.gov/2017944047

CONTENTS

1

ADA LOVELACE

Ada Lovelace was a scientist in the early 1800s. She was one of the first female scientists. At that time, women were not encouraged to learn science. However, some women, like Ada Lovelace, did anyway.

Lovelace was the daughter of the poet Lord Byron and part of the English upper class. She had social and educational opportunities that most girls during her time did not. Her mother, Annabella Byron, was well educated and wanted the same for her daughter.

Lord Byron was known to have an unstable personality. Lady Byron was afraid Ada might have inherited her

"Understand well as I may, my comprehension can only be an **infinitesimal** fraction of all I want to understand."

–Ada Lovelace

Ada Lovelace was the first person to suggest using computers for tasks other than mathematics.

father's emotional problems. She believed education was the way to keep Ada's mind strong and her emotions calm.

Lovelace was unusual in both the amount and type of her education. She also had a professional career when most women didn't. Lovelace had long-term associations with another female scientist, Mary Somerville, and the mathematician and inventor Charles Babbage. It was through her work with Babbage that Lovelace would become known as the first computer **programmer**.

2
FAMOUS FATHER

Augusta Ada Byron was born on December 10, 1815, in London, England. She went by her middle name. Ada was the daughter of the poet Lord Byron. His full name was George Gordon Byron and he was a baron in the British **aristocracy**. Ada's mother was Anne Isabella Milbanke. Anne Isabella was known as Annabella.

When Annabella met Lord Byron, he was famous for his poetry. He was charming but moody. Annabella was unsure whether she wanted to marry him. She rejected his first proposal. However, she accepted when he asked again.

Annabella and Byron were married in January 1815. Their relationship was difficult from the start. In fact, Byron was late for his own wedding! Byron was unable to focus on being a husband and father. He and Lady Byron separated a few weeks after Ada was born.

Lord Byron is considered one of the greatest British poets in history. He is most famous for the poems "Don Juan" and "She Walks in Beauty."

Byron left England when Ada was a few months old. He lived the rest of his life in Italy and Greece. Ada stayed in England with her mother. She never knew her father. He died in 1824, when Ada was eight years old.

3
EARLY EDUCATION

Ada and her mother did not have a close relationship. When Ada was little, she often stayed with Lady Byron's mother, Lady Judith Milbanke. Ada's grandmother died when she was still very young. After that, Ada was mostly raised by **governesses**.

Although Lady Byron didn't spend much time with Ada, she wrote often. Lady Byron was especially concerned about Ada's education. She believed that Lord Byron was unstable and didn't want Ada to be like her father.

Lady Byron was well educated and a gifted mathematician. She thought that a similar education would keep Ada from becoming overly emotional. Lady Byron felt that Ada's mind would remain healthy if she studied science, mathematics, and **logic**.

Ada began learning these subjects when she was four years old. She was taught at home by **tutors**. From the start, Ada showed great skill with math and language.

Besides math and science, Ada also studied music. She could play the piano, violin, and harp.

4

TERRIFIC TUTORS

Ada's education was unusual in England at that time. An upper-class girl like Ada was usually taught by her **governess** rather than **tutors**. She would learn skills such as playing the piano, drawing, and flower arranging. She might even learn French. The goal was to learn skills that would help a young lady attract a husband. But Lady Byron set Ada on a different path.

Lady Byron hired William Frend and William King to teach Ada math and science. Frend had been Lady Byron's tutor when she was a girl. King was the family's doctor.

Ada also studied with Mary Somerville. Somerville was a Scottish mathematician and astronomer. She was one of the first women admitted into the Royal Astronomical Society. As Ada grew older, Somerville became her **mentor** and friend. She encouraged Ada's studies. They frequently discussed mathematics together.

Later, Ada studied under Augustus De Morgan, who was a professor at University College in London. He was a mathematician and **logician**. He taught Ada logic and was impressed by her ability.

Mary Somerville was a brilliant scientist. She also strongly supported women's education and voting rights.

5

FIGURING OUT FLIGHT

Ada was fascinated by machines. She read journals about machines and studied drawings of them. She also studied the structure of birds' wings. In 1828, she began designing her own flying machine. She was just 12 years old.

Ada already knew how to work like a scientist. She conducted research. She studied the wings and bodies of birds. She drew plans showing how her machine would work. She tested wings in different sizes using different materials.

Ada thought her machine could be powered by a steam engine. She included a compass for navigation. Ada pictured the machine looking like a horse. A

DID YOU KNOW?

In 1842, English **engineer** William Henson patented an aerial steam carriage. He built it with the help of fellow engineer John Stringfellow. They were unaware of Ada's work from 15 years earlier. But their invention was similar in some ways to her design.

Despite Annabella's efforts, Ada retained some of her father's influence. Ada called herself a poetical scientist.

person would sit on its back. The machine would fly using large wings moved by the steam engine inside.

Ada collected her plans and notes in a book titled *Flyology*. Ada never actually built her flying machine, though. Her mother encouraged Ada to concentrate on her studies of math and science.

6

MEANINGFUL MEETING

Somerville introduced Ada to Charles Babbage in 1833. Babbage was a mathematician and **engineer**. This meeting was the beginning of a lifelong working relationship between the two. Babbage was impressed by Ada's intelligence. They often corresponded about mathematics, **logic**, and other subjects.

Mathematicians at that time looked up answers to problems in tables of numbers. These tables were handwritten and often had errors. In the 1820s, Babbage designed a machine that would do two things. It would perform calculations correctly. Then it would print the answers.

DID YOU KNOW?

In the 1800s, people assumed men were naturally smarter than women. Women were thought to be too delicate for subjects such as math and science. Some doctors even believed too much education would damage a woman's ability to have children.

Babbage never completed the Difference Engine. But in 2002 the Science Museum in London built a model based on his plans.

Babbage worked on a **prototype**. He called it a Difference Engine. He invited Ada to watch it work. The machine could only calculate addition problems. This meant it could not be used for every type of arithmetic. But Ada was fascinated by it. She asked Babbage for a copy of the Difference Engine's plans. She studied the plans to learn how the machine worked.

7

MAKING TIME FOR MARRIAGE

Ada took time out from her studies to start a family. In 1835, she married William King, 8th Baron King. He was ten years older than Ada. In 1838, King was made the first Earl of Lovelace. Ada became the Countess of Lovelace. She was known simply as Ada Lovelace.

King and Lovelace had three children. Their two sons were named Byron and Ralph Gordon. Their daughter was named Anne Isabella after Ada's mother.

BETTING ON HORSES

In the 1840s, Lovelace developed a love of horses and gambling. Lovelace and Babbage tried creating mathematical methods for picking race winners. But the methods didn't work. The failures left Lovelace owing a lot of money. She had to secretly sell the Lovelace family jewels to pay what she owed.

Lovelace continued her studies while raising her children. She even hired a private tutor, Augustus De Morgan, to teach her advanced mathematics.

Lovelace and King had a loving marriage. King's support of his wife's work was uncommon. Most husbands at the time expected their wives to focus only on home and family. But King accepted Lovelace's desire to continue her math and science studies.

8
ANALYTICAL ENGINE

Lovelace was fortunate to know people who respected her intelligence. She knew the scientist Michael Faraday and the author Charles Dickens. She was also acquainted with Sir David Brewster, who invented the **kaleidoscope**.

In 1834, Charles Babbage began working on a new calculating machine. He called it the **Analytical** Engine. This machine could do more than addition. Unlike the Difference Engine, the Analytical Engine could perform all four arithmetic operations. These are addition, subtraction, multiplication and division. The Analytical Engine was a general computing machine.

Babbage's machine was controlled by punch cards. These were paper cards with holes punched in them. The holes represented numbers and instructions. When fed into the machine, the positions of the holes told the machine what to do. A similar punch card system was

Although he didn't complete his projects, Charles Babbage is often considered the father of the computer.

already being used by weaving looms to direct the pattern of fabrics.

In the early 1840s, Babbage lectured in Italy about the **Analytical** Engine. While there, Babbage met Italian **engineer**, Luigi Menabrea. Menabrea wrote an article about the Analytical Engine. Its title was "Elements of

Bernoulli numbers are a series of numbers that are calculated by a mathematical **formula**. Swiss mathematician Jakob Bernoulli developed the system in the late 1600s. Bernoulli numbers are important in advanced mathematics and number theory.

Charles Babbage's **Analytical** Machine." The article was written in French and published in a Swiss journal.

Lovelace knew French well. Babbage asked her to translate Menabrea's article from French to English. Through her correspondence with Babbage, Lovelace knew more than Menabrea about the machine. She expanded on Menabrea's writing. And she updated some information that had changed since Menabrea wrote the article. She completed her translation in 1843.

Babbage reviewed the translation and was delighted with it. He invited Lovelace to add her own notes to Menabrea's article. Lovelace had a deep understanding of the Analytical Engine. Her notes made the article three times longer!

Lovelace labeled her notes A through G. In these notes, she wrote mathematical formulas that explained how the

Diagram for the computation by the Engine of the Numbers of Bernoulli. See Note G. (page 722 *et seq.*)

The diagram is a large fold-out table of working variables for the Bernoulli number computation, with columns for Data, Working Variables, and Result Variables, and rows giving the indication of change, statement of results, and numerical values such as $2n$, $2n-1$, $2n+1$, $\frac{2n-1}{2n+1}$, $-\frac{1}{2}\cdot\frac{2n-1}{2n+1}=A_0$, A_1, $B_1 A_1$, A_3, $B_3 A_3$, and the result variables B_1, B_3, etc.

Lovelace created a chart to compute Bernoulli numbers and included it in her translated article.

Analytical Engine could perform calculations. Note G included an **algorithm** for calculating Bernoulli numbers. Bernoulli numbers are a **complex** system. Lovelace wanted to show that these, or any, numbers could be correctly calculated by the Analytical Engine.

9

PROGRAMMING PIONEER

Lovelace's translation of Menabrea's article was published in the English science journal *Scientific Memoirs* in 1843. She signed it with only her initials, A.A.L. There were several possible reasons for this. One was that at the time, it was standard for translators of works to be unnamed. Also, it was frowned on for **aristocrats**, especially women, to have professions. Finally, women's ideas weren't considered as important as men's. So, many professional women used their initials.

The value of Lovelace's notes on the article was not recognized until more than 100 years later. In 1953, English scientist B.V. Bowden republished Lovelace's notes in his book, *Faster Than Thought: A Symposium on Digital Computing Machines*. It was only then that the importance of her work became known.

Babbage thought of the **Analytical** Engine only in terms of making mathematical calculations. But Lovelace saw other possibilities as well. The Bernoulli **algorithm** in

The Jacquard loom played a large part in Lovelace's thinking. She wrote, "The Analytical Engine weaves mathematical patterns just as the Jacquard loom weaves flowers and leaves."

Whether she was the first programmer or not, Lovelace is still considered a brilliant mathematician by many. Her work continues to inspire female and male scientists.

Note G showed that Lovelace understood that any type of data could be represented by numbers. This would allow the data to be entered into the engine. Then the engine could process the data using commands. Although computers would not be invented for many years, these ideas represent what a computer **program** is.

Lovelace and Babbage exchanged ideas and work while Lovelace was translating Menabrea's article. Lovelace is credited by most as having authored the Bernoulli **algorithm**. For this reason, she is widely considered to have been the first computer programmer. Her understanding of the **Analytical** Engine was the first step toward the modern computer. She is sometimes referred to as the "prophet of the computer age."

Not all scholars agree that Lovelace was the first computer programmer. Some credit Babbage. Babbage had written some unpublished algorithms for the Analytical Engine back in 1836 and 1837. Some scholars say that, though Lovelace perfected these algorithms and corrected bugs in them, they were not her original work.

10

EARLY END

/////////////

Ada Lovelace suffered from many illnesses throughout her life. As a child, she had headaches bad enough to affect her vision. As a teenager, she had **measles**, which left her bedridden for a year. Lovelace also got **cholera** in 1837. And she often had breathing problems.

Then in 1851, Lovelace learned she had **cancer**. She died on November 27, 1852. Though Lovelace hadn't known her father, she had been interested in him and his writing. At her request, she was buried next to Lord Byron. Their final resting place is a family vault inside the Church of Saint Mary Magdalene in Hucknall, England.

ONGOING INFLUENCE

In the 1970s, the US Department of Defense developed a new computer language. It was named "Ada" in Lovelace's honor. Ada is used in health care, transportation, finance, space, and more.

Ada Lovelace's life wasn't very long, but it was full of important accomplishments that are remembered today. Since 2009, Ada Lovelace Day has been celebrated each year. On this day, people learn and write about influential women in STEM. Girls and women find **role models** in science, **technology**, **engineering**, and math. One of these role models is Ada Lovelace. She was a STEM pioneer.

In 2015, the Church of St. Mary Magdalene held an event to celebrate Lovelace's two-hundredth birthday.

TIMELINE

1815
Augusta Ada Byron is born on December 10 in London, England.

1828
Ada designs a flying machine. She collects her notes about it in a book titled *Flyology*.

1833
Mary Somerville introduces Ada to Charles Babbage. Ada becomes fascinated with his Difference Engine.

1834
Charles Babbage begins work on the Analytical Engine.

1835
Ada marries William King, 8th Baron King.

1838

Ada's husband is made Earl of Lovelace. Ada becomes known as Ada Lovelace.

1840s

Charles Babbage lectures in Italy about the Analytical Engine. Luigi Menabrea writes an article in French about the lecture.

1843

Lovelace completes her English translation of Menabrea's article. She adds extensive notes of her own.

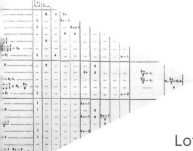

1852

Lovelace dies from cancer on November 27.

1953

Lovelace's translation is republished. People realize that her notes contain the first computer program.

GLOSSARY

algorithm—a set of steps that are followed in order to solve a mathematical problem or to complete a computer process.

analytical—related to the process or instance of examining something closely to learn the nature and relationship of its parts.

aristocracy—people who are born into a high social class. A member of such a class is an aristocrat.

cancer—any of a group of often deadly diseases marked by harmful changes in the normal growth of cells. Cancer can spread and destroy healthy tissues and organs.

cholera—a disease of the intestines marked by severe diarrhea.

complex—having many parts, details, ideas, or functions.

engineering—the application of science and mathematics to design and create useful structures, products, or systems. A person who does this is an engineer.

formula—a mathematical fact or rule expressed in letters and symbols.

governess—a woman who teaches and trains a child especially in a private home.

infinitesimal—extremely small.

kaleidoscope—a tube with mirrors and loose pieces of colored glass inside one end that shows many different patterns when viewed through the other end.

logic—the science dealing with rules of correct reasoning and with proof by reasoning. Someone who studies logic is a logician.

measles—a disease marked by a fever and small, red spots on the skin.

mentor—a trusted adviser or guide.

program—a set of instructions or commands for a computer to follow. Someone who writes or inputs a program is a programmer.

prototype—a first full-scale and usually functional form of a new type or design of a product or machine.

role model—a person whose behavior serves as a standard for others to follow.

technology—the use of science in solving problems.

tutor—a person who teaches a student privately.

ONLINE RESOURCES

Booklinks
NONFICTION NETWORK
FREE! ONLINE NONFICTION RESOURCES

To learn more about Ada Lovelace, visit **abdobooklinks.com**. These links are routinely monitored and updated to provide the most current information available.

INDEX